SACRED SCROLLS IN PLAIN ENGLISH

Sacred Scrolls
in Plain English

THE BOOKS OF ECCLESIASTES, SONG OF SONGS,
LAMENTATIONS, RUTH, AND PROVERBS

English Rendition by
AARON LICHTENSTEIN

URIM PUBLICATIONS
Jerusalem • New York

Sacred Scrolls in Plain English:
The Books of Ecclesiastes, Song of Songs,
Lamentations, Ruth, and Proverbs
by Aaron Lichtenstein

Copyright © 2018 Aaron Lichtenstein

Typeset by Ariel Walden

Printed in USA

First Edition

ISBN 978-1-60280-312-1

Urim Publications
P.O. Box 52287
Jerusalem 9152102
Israel
www.UrimPublications.com

Library of Congress Cataloging-in-Publication Data
Names: Lichtenstein, Aaron, translator.
Title: Sacred scrolls in plain English : the books of Ecclesiastes, Song of
    Songs, Lamentations, Ruth, and Proverbs / English rendition by Aaron
    Lichtenstein.
Other titles: Bible. Five Scrolls. English. 2018. | Bible. Proverbs. English.
    2018. | Bible. Psalms. English. 2018. | Bible. Samuel, 2nd. English. 2018. |
    Bible. Pentateuch. English. 2018.
Description: First Edition. | Jerusalem ; New York : Urim Publications,
    [2018]
Identifiers: LCCN 2017057645 | ISBN 9781602803121 (hardback)
Subjects: | BISAC: RELIGION / Judaism / Sacred Writings. | RELIGION /
    Biblical Criticism & Interpretation / Old Testament.
Classification: LCC BS1309.A3 L53 2018 | DDC 223/.05209—dc23 LC
    record available at https://lccn.loc.gov/2017057645

Contents

I.
FIVE SACRED BOOKS

The Book of Ecclesiastes
Koheleth

The words of Koheleth, son of David, king of Jerusalem:

MEANINGLESS NOTHING, SAYS Koheleth, it is a meaningless nothing because everything is nothing. What does a person get for all the work he does under the sun? The generation passes on and a new generation arrives, but the world is unchanged. Thus the sun rises and the sun sets, but circles in orbit to shine over there. It moves toward south, then circles back to north. Just so, the wind blows round and round, to circle back unto itself. So the rivers flow to where they flowed from. Indeed all science is a bore, because a person cannot explain it, his eyes cannot see enough of it, and his ears can never hear all about it. Rather, whatever was yet will be, and whatever was done is what is being done, for there is nothing new under the sun. Someone may say: See this is new. No, it was already there during the eternity which preceded us. For we have no memory of the beginnings just as there will be no remembrance of the present, even if this is the end.

I Koheleth have been king of Israel in Jerusalem, and have devoted myself to intelligently examining all that is happening here under the horizon. However, this is a sad undertaking with which mankind has been burdened by God. I have observed all the goings-on which go on under the sun and have found them all worthless and depressing, like a mistake which cannot be fixed or a shortfall which does not add up.

Still, I said to myself: Here, I am wiser and more knowledgeable than those who preceded me in Jerusalem, where I absorbed much wisdom and knowledge. So let me devote myself to an understanding of wisdom and to identifying foolishness. Yet I knew this to be a dismal idea, since an abundance of wisdom leads to anger and an abundance of knowledge invites agitation.

Chapter Two

INSTEAD, I SAID to myself, let me wallow in delight and be happy. But, of course, this too is futile, for I consider laughter foolish and merriment accomplishes nothing. Still, I persisted and began to ply myself with wines, as all the while my heart was led by wisdom, for defining folly and for seeking what is worthwhile for people to do during their few days on this side of heaven. I embarked on great projects. I built houses, I planted vineyards, gardens, orchards, planted varied fruit trees, and dug reservoirs for watering forests of trees. I bought slaves and maid-servants, then invited guests. I owned more cattle and sheep in

Jerusalem than anyone before. I collected silver and gold and the treasures precious to monarchs and nations. I got me tenors and sopranos, amusements for the gentlemen, beauty queens and ladies of the court. I did it better and more than anyone preceding me in Jerusalem, but my wisdom yet stood by me. Whatever I saw, I did not deny myself. I did not hold back from any enjoyment, and I enjoyed myself with my projects, expecting this to be the upshot of all my labors. But standing back to evaluate what I accomplished with these works, I realized them to be empty, presumptuous, and unworthy facing the sun. So I turned once more to defining wisdom and identifying foolish folly – and who can compete with what a king has already accomplished.

I believe that wisdom is better than folly, in the same way that light is better than darkness. A wise man sees with open eyes, while the fool moves in the dark, but I am aware how both end up the same way. And I said to myself: What happens to this fool happens to me also, so what does my wisdom do for me? I considered this a terrible downer, that there is no remembrance of the wise over the fool, since everything is forgotten eventually. How is it that the wise dies like the fool?

I began to despise life and hated everything there was under the sun as meaningless and presumption. I hated all those projects which I had initiated, also because I was to leave them for someone who follows me – and who knows if he be wise or foolish – to lord it over what I had created, struggling and envisioning under this sun. This too is disheartening. I tried to forget the great works that I had undertaken under the sun.

For here was a man who labored with wisdom, knowledge and cunning, but it all will go to someone who did not fashion it. There is this huge injustice. In the end, what does a person get for all his efforts which he invests under the sun? He becomes indisposed and upset during the day and then has a sleepless night. Dreadful. So it would be best for a person to eat and drink and be happy with his job – and I realize that even this would be a gift from God. My eating and my disposition becomes my own. God gives the person He likes wisdom, understanding and happiness, while He has the sinner gather things for transfer to whomever God likes. This is dispiriting as well.

Chapter Three

THERE IS A time for everything and an eventual use for each facet here under the sky:

As there is a time for birth and a time of death, so is there a time for planting and a time for uprooting.

As there is a time to kill and a time to heal, so is there a time to demolish and a time to build.

As there is a time to cry and a time to laugh, so is there a time for eulogy and a time for dance.

As there is a time to clear stones and a time to collect stones, so is there a time for embracing and a time for rejection.

As there is a time to gather and a time to dump, so is there a time for conservation and a time for waste.

As there is a time to rip open and a time to sew closed, so is there a time to quiet down and a time to speak out.

As there is a time to love and a time to hate, so is there a time for war and a time for peace.

What then is the merit of all human endeavors? I see what it is that God has presented man for resolution: He has presented each thing to be right in its time. Beyond this, He has put the idea of eternity in their imaginations, without which the people would not strive to comprehend God's workings from beginning to end. And I know that the best thing is to rejoice and be happy with one's life. And any man who could eat and drink and enjoy his lifelong labor has received a gift from God. And I know that whatever God does is permanent, without additions or subtractions, and that all are created by God in order for them to recognize Him. What is was already, and what will be was too, while God deals with the present.

I also noticed that under the sun the courthouse is a place for wickedness, that where you expect justice you get abuse. I thought in my heart, God shall eventually judge the innocent and the guilty, for there is a right time for every object and action down there.

Then I said to myself, God has endowed the humans but they see themselves as mere animals because what happens to humans happens to animals. Both these and those die, and human life is as futile as the animal's. Both end up in the same place, both coming from the earth and returning to the earth. For who can demonstrate that the soul of men rises up to heaven while the spirit of animals sinks into the ground? Thus, I confirm that the best thing for a man to do is rejoice in whatever he does – this is the only thing he has – for nobody can demonstrate to him what will happen thereafter.

Chapter Four

I TOOK A HARD look at all the violence being committed under the sun. Here are the tears of the oppressed with no one to sympathize, with no defense against the oppressors and no consolation. So I praise the dead, those who died already instead of those who are still alive for the moment. Even better are those who never were, who never witnessed the evils committed under the sun. For I see how jealousy is at the root of men's enterprise and maneuvering – a sad waste.

A fool wrings his hands and eats his flesh.

One handful in tranquility is better than two handfuls with strain and anguish.

I had a look at yet another loser under the sun: Alone, by

himself, no son, no brother, he works endlessly, is never satisfied with his wealth, always striving and never allowing himself to enjoy – a vain and grim situation.

Better two together than one alone, as the two can profit nicely at their business. If they slip, each can help the other up, but when a loner trips there will be no one to pick him up. Just so, two sleeping together will feel warm, but this loner cannot get warm. Then, if one is mugged, the two can resist, and a triple-stranded rope does not snap readily.

Better a powerless, smart youth than an old foolish king who can no longer take care. Even coming from prison he may become the next king. During his eventual reign too a worthier lad may be born. I can visualize the multitudes that march in the sun with this second monarch. One could not have counted the multitudes that preceded him, and these masses now will not remain loyal – here are futility and disappointment.

Beware when you approach the House of God. Obey, instead of bringing sacrifices like those fools who cannot understand even their own wickedness.

Chapter Five

CONTROL YOURSELF, DON'T rush into saying something before God. For God is in heaven and you are an earthling, so be brief; dreams and fools go on and on. And when you make a pledge before God do not delay payment – such fools are not needed – deliver what you pledge. It is better not to promise than to promise and not give. Do not let your tongue jeopardize your whole body, and do not be telling an Angel that it was a mistake, because God may react to your words by calling in your inventory. Instead of dreams, stupidities and speeches, be afraid of God.

Don't be shocked if you witness oppression of the poor and miscarriage of justice in the land. For there are yet higher-ups who are responsible for it. Each of them wants a cut and even a king can use a well-cultivated field.

Whoever loves money will never be satisfied with money, and anyone who craves popularity will never get enough of it.

As the bank roll increases so do the spending partners, and what does the owner get but the sight of his cash flow.

A working man sleeps soundly, whatever his supper, but the wealthy cannot sleep from overeating.

I witnessed a sickening evil here under the sun, regarding wealth accumulated to harm its possessor: Should he lose his riches in a disaster he will suddenly have nothing – even to support a baby boy. He returns to the grave as stripped as when he emerged from his mother's belly with nothing to show for lifelong labors. This is a revolting injustice, in that he exits as he entered and that his effort was in vain, having eaten his suppers in the dark of the night after much annoyance, sickness and rage. So what I advise is for you to eat and drink and whistle while you work during your lifetime under the sun, for this is your share in the few days which God grants you. And anyone who attains wealth and manages to consume his part of it and to enjoy his labor, is the recipient of a gift from God.

Few will remember his life, but God can testify that he lived happily.

Chapter Six

I TOOK NOTE OF another tragedy which weighs heavily on mankind. Here is a person to whom God gives riches, property, respect and who does not lack for anything which he desires. There comes along a stranger who takes all of it over, not letting the original owner benefit. The futility here is sickening. For should a man give birth to a hundred children and live long years, but not satisfy his soul – perhaps not even getting a proper burial – I say that an aborted fetus is better off. The fetus comes in vain, departs in darkness, with the dark beclouding its name, never catching sight of the sun and never knowing anything. It is better off than this man. And what if the man had lived a thousand years twice over but achieved no satisfaction, do all not end up in the same place?

A person's endless labor is for his next meal, and his soul too never becomes sated.

Is the wise better off than the fool? No pauper can contend with life's challenges.

Superficiality is safer than soul-searching, everything being useless and oppressive.

Man's state of affairs is long established: If he is human he is unable to overcome forces stronger than himself, for there are numerous elements that pile helplessness onto humanity.

And who can tell a man what is the good life for him to pursue during his short, shadowy existence, and tell him what happens after he departs from under the sun?

Chapter Seven

B ETTER A GOOD reputation than good ointment, and the time of death than the time of birth.

Better to go to a house of mourning than to a house party, for the former is a person's ultimate destination and the living can take it to heart.

Better anger than jollity, for after expressing the anger you feel better.

The wise are calm in a home of bereavement, and a fool in a home of merriment.

Better to hear the rebuke of the wise than to attend a fool's song fest. The fool's jokes are like the crackle of thorns in the fireplace – all meaningless. Poking fun distracts the wise man and contaminates his generous heart.

Better to evaluate at a project's end than its beginning, and better lowly modesty than high pride.

Do not rush into anger, for anger belongs to the bosom of fools. Do not ask: What happened to the good old days which were better than these? It is not your wisdom that asks thus.

Better wisdom when allied with wealth, with wherewithal to confront the sun. When protected by intelligence, money and understanding, wisdom can sustain its master.

Study God's creations, since who can fix what He breaks. On a good day accept the good and on a bad day understand how God juxtaposed one and the other, so that people cannot second-guess Him. I have seen it all during my lean years: The righteous perishing in his piety and the evildoer persevering in his wickedness. So don't be extremely pious and don't be overly wise – why should you suffer? And don't sin away – why should you die before your time? Be aware of these and those, since a reverence for God emerges from their totality.

Wisdom can bolster a wise person better than ten city chiefs. For no pious person can be as innocent as to do no wrong. So do not take note of everything that is said, lest you overhear your servant cursing you. And you well know the numerous occasions on which you cursed others.

These things I tested intelligently, for I wanted to be wise, but it outdistances me by far. Far as can be and deeper than one can dig. I had committed myself to comprehend, to investigate, and to research wisdom and science. Likewise, to comprehend evil, foolishness, stupidity and pandemonium. I discovered here that worse than death is the wife whose essence is traps, snares, and whose hands are chains. Anyone who finds favor in the eyes of God will avoid her while the sinner will be caught.

Then I concluded this too: That bit by bit can add up to the grand total. But what I especially wanted to uncover I could not find: Only the real man in a thousand did I find, and a real woman in even a thousand I did not find. Aside from this, I established that God has fashioned an upright human species, but they pursue a mess of twists and turns.

Chapter Eight

WHO CAN COMPARE to a wise man who knows the answer; his wisdom lights up his face and banishes coarseness.

I follow a king's orders, as if sworn by God. Be quick to make way for him. Do not join demonstrators, for he can do what he wants. The king's word is law, and no one can tell him otherwise. One who obeys has no problems, and a smart heart can tell what is right and timely. Everything has a right time, beyond which great dangers lurk for mankind. For a man does not know what will happen and when it happens nobody tells him about it. A person does not control his spirit of life, there are no supermen on a day of death, no survivors during a slaughter, and no violence can save its perpetrator.

I witnessed under the sun how men tyrannize men out of spite. I also saw scoundrels given a funeral and burial on sacred ground, with no mention of the city-wide crimes they committed. It is because retribution does not come swiftly that the evil-hearted continue their evil deeds, since a sinner can sin a hundred fold and survive. I know of course that goodness comes to those who fear God and revere Him, while no good reaches the wicked who do not fear God in their short, shadowy existence. But there is a dreadful wrong on earth when the righteous are punished like lawbreakers and the scoundrels receive benefits like saints – awful. So I recommend gaiety, there not being anything under the sun more worthwhile than feasting, drinking and merriment, to accompany a person's labors in the lifetime which God allows him.

Chapter Nine

WHILE I WAS involved in defining intelligence and in examining what transpires globally, for days and sleepless nights, I concluded that it was really impossible for a person to review God's work and interpret the universe; no matter how hard he tried, even a genius would fail.

But I did think about how it is that the intelligent elite as well as their slaves rest equally in God's hands, for no person understands why he loves or hates or anything. All function the same way, the righteous, the evildoer, the innocent, the pure, the dirty, the worshiper, the abstainer, the good, the bad, the oath-taker, as well as the one who eschews oaths.

Then there is this problem with what goes on under the sun, that everyone ends up the same way, prompting men's hearts to fill with perdition and craziness, during their lives before death. Yet, anyone grasping for life still has hope, since a living dog is better than a dead lion.

For the living know they are going to die, while the dead know nothing, can claim nothing, and are soon forgotten. Their loves, their hates, their jealousies are no more and they play no role in what goes on under the sun. You, go ahead indulge yourself with dinners, drink your wine lustily, for God accepts what you are doing. Live your life with the woman you love during the baffling existence which God grants you under the sun. Do whatever you find possible to accomplish with your energies, since there will be no action, no planning, no information and no intelligence in the grave that you are headed for.

I turned to ponder why, here under the sun, it is not the swift who win a race, nor the strong who win the war, nor the wise who have food, nor the intelligent who are rich, nor the witty popular. Rather, chance and accident afflict everyone. A person does not even know when his time is up, like fish caught in a waiting net, like a bird in a trap. Just so do humans become undone by a mishap which befalls them suddenly.

I also took note under the sun how impressive wisdom can be. Here was a small village which was besieged by a mighty king who surrounded it with high embankments. But there was in the village a clever poor man who saved the village by virtue of his wisdom. They soon forgot this poor man but I said to myself, wisdom is better than power, although they look down and brush aside the intelligence of the lowly. The whispered words of the wise are more convincing than the shouted orders of fools. Wisdom is stronger than armament, yet one miscreant can ruin a good thing.

Chapter Ten

POISON FLEAS CAN spoil wholesome oils, just as a pinch of stupidity can spoil respected wisdom. The heart of the wise is right on, the heart of the fool is left out. Wherever the fool may go he advertises that he is a fool at heart.

If the boss is angry with you remain calm, for stroking can pacify nasty complaints.

I noticed another wrong under the sun as devastating as a

mistake made on high: Mediocrites riding high while million-aires bite the dust. My eyes have seen slaves on stallions with princes trudging along like servants.

He who digs holes may himself fall in, and he who removes fences may himself suffer a snakebite. The hewer of stones may be injured by them, as the chopper of wood will be hurt by wood.

If the ax is flimsy and its blade dull but the soldier is fit, perhaps cleverness will do the rest.

If a snake should bite without its hiss, then a gossiper should not need his murmur.

It is a pleasure when a sage opens his mouth, but the lips of a fool chew you out – he begins in foolishness and ends with mischief.

The simpleton pronounces on every matter, although no man knows what will happen, and when it happens after he is gone who can tell him about it. The simpleton's confusion wears him out so that he cannot manage to return to where he started from.

Woe, you nation whose king is a follower and whose aris-tocracy party from morning. Lucky, you nation whose king is a free man and whose aristocracy party when appropriate – for authority, not as drunks.

The lazy will let the ceiling fall in, just as the inept will have a leaking roof.

They dine for hilarity, drink for good cheer, and money is their ubiquitous answer.

Don't even think about cursing royalty and don't curse a

rich man even in your private chamber, because a bird in flight
may spread the word, and anyone with wings will tell.

Chapter Eleven

P LANT YOUR GRAIN under rain, for in time you will get it
back. Diverse into seven or eight shares, for you cannot
time a crash. Saying, maybe if the clouds fill to pour rain on
my field, is like saying, maybe a tree will topple down South or
maybe up North. It makes no difference where the tree topples
it is there, but if you wait for the winds and look to the clouds,
you will have no harvest. Just as you cannot forecast a breeze,
or spot a bone in a bloated belly, you cannot fathom an act of
God. Therefore plant your seedlings early, plant again late;
since you can't guess which will blossom, or both. Enjoy the
light, your eyes relish the sunlight. As long as a person lives
let him enjoy himself throughout, being cognizant of that day
of endless darkness. So boy, enjoy your youth, be enthusiastic
in your boyhood, follow your heart and your desires, while
remembering that God will have you judged for what you do.
Rid your heart of anger and your body of lust, as both boyhood
and adulthood are vain.

Chapter Twelve

REMEMBER YOUR CREATOR while you are young,
Before the sad days come, when
You have years you could do without.
Before darkness covers sunlight, moon and stars,
When there are clouds there without rain,
On the day when the rib cage shrinks,
And the two strong arms tremble,
Grinding stops as the molars decay,
And vision dims in the peepholes,
The outside openings get clogged,
While the inner process stills,
The chirping birds are too loud,
But the throat chokes on a song,
Afraid to stand, to trip in walking,
Ambition gone, energy lost, passions void,
For man is advancing toward eternal rest,
With his mourners gathering in the street.
Before the silver spine-cord snaps,
And the golden globe is smashed,
The container cracks at the fountain,
And the wheel drops back down the well,
Whereupon the flesh turns to earth again,
While the spirit returns to the Lord who gave it.
Meaningless nothing, declared Koheleth,
Everything is nothing . . .

As Koheleth became increasingly wise, he taught the people wisdom, discussing, researching and framing many proverbs. Koheleth strove to gather bright sayings, intelligent texts, and profound truths. The words of the sages are like pointers, like guardrails arranged by one master. Beyond these, my son, beware since there is no end to publishing how-to books which leave you bored. When everything becomes clear, the bottom line is fear God and observe His commandments, for only this matters to mankind. Then God will have everyone judged for his secret deeds, be they good or bad.

The Song of Songs of Solomon

Kiss me, kiss with kisses of the lips
because your friendship is more
compelling than wine. Even a whiff
of your scent enthralls, its aroma
wafting far, therefore do all the
girls love you. Take me with you,
let's run off, take me to your
majestic apartment where we can
rejoice, to enjoy your comradery
more than wine, for our love is right.

"O daughters of Jerusalem, I may be
dark but still am beautiful, like a
Bedouwin tent or Solomon's tapestries.
Don't consider me a darkee – it is only
a suntan – because my stepbrothers
forced me out to tend the vineyards
and it was not even my own vineyard
that I tended."

Tell me, love of my life, where you
will be shepherding this afternoon, for
why should I be passing by your
colleague's flocks like a vulture?

O beautiful woman, you need not
know, just follow your own sheep
over the grassland where you graze
your kids. My darling, you present like
a thoroughbred in Pharaoh's cavalry.
Your cheeks are sweet love doves,
your neck like a colonnade –
we must buy you a gold necklace
spangled with silver.

With my prince still at table, my perfume
swirls its fragrance. My beau is a bundle
of myrtle coming to rest at my breasts.
My beau is like a spice-cluster grown
in the orchards of En-gedi.

You are beautiful, my dear, your eyes
are like doves.

You are handsome, my love, and so wonderful.
The bedding is fresh, the walls of our
house are cedar and our furnishings
are cypress.

Chapter Two

I am a lily of Sharon, a rose of the
valley.

> Like a rose amid the thorns, so stands
> my darling among the maidens.

Like an apple tree amidst the forest trees, so stands
my love, amidst the lads; under its shade I grew
passionate, remaining to find its
fruit sweet to my palate. Revive me
with liquor, calm me with the apples,
for I am lovesick. Let him bring
me to the wine shed to proclaim his
love for me, with his left hand at
my head and his right hand hugging me.
"O daughters of Jerusalem, swear to
me, by the does or gazelles of the wild,
that you not arouse this passion until
it may be realized."

Listen, it is the voice of my love.
He comes skipping along the mountains,
bounding over the hills. My love
arrives like a stag or young gazelle,
standing now at the building, peering
from the window, looking through
the slats. My love calls to me, saying:

My beautiful darling, rise up and
get going. The winter is over, the
rains are no more. Buds are everywhere,
happy days are here. The coos of
the turtledoves are heard all about, the
fig tree has produced its fruit, and the
grapevine blossoms with its fragrance.
Arise and come away, my beautiful
darling, get going. My lovebird,
as in a cleft of a rock up on a
cliff, show yourself to me. Let me
hear your voice because your voice
is mellow and you are good looking.
We shall catch us those foxes, those
little foxes that tear about the
vineyard while our vineyard is in
bloom.

I am my love's and my love
is mine, as he goes shepherding
amid the roses. But my love, before
this day ends and its shadows
disappear, turn you once again
into the likes of a stag or young
gazelle upon distant heights.

Chapter Three

At night in my bed I sought the
love of my life. I searched but
found him not. I would get up to
circle the city, through alleys and
avenues in search of my love.

I searched but found him not. I
was met by the watchmen who circle
the city; I asked: Have you seen
my love? Just as I pass them
I found my love. I take hold of
him and not let him go until I lead
him to my mother's house, to the
bedroom where I was conceived.

"O daughters of Jerusalem, I adjure
you, by the deer and gazelles of
the wild, that you not bring up
nor stir up this love until it can
be realized."

Who is this coming out of the desert in a burst of
cloud, all made up with myrrh, incense, and a beautician's
cosmetics? There too is the couch of Solomon, supported
by sixty soldiers of Israel, each a veteran swordsman with
his sword at his side to defend against the dangers of the

night. Solomon made himself a coach of timber from the Lebanon, with sides of silver, its ceiling of gold, its flooring of purple wool, all decked out with love by the daughters of Jerusalem. O daughters of Jerusalem, come here and behold King Solomon wearing a crown which his mother gave him for his wedding day, this day of heartfelt joy.

Chapter Four

My fiancée, you are lovely, your
eyes are like doves behind your
curls, your hair like a flock that
streams down Mount Gilead. Your
teeth, like a family of ewes after
their bath, perfectly matched and
without a spot. Your lips are a
strand of scarlet, with your mouth
well proportioned, and your forehead
like a section of pomegranate seen
from behind your curls. Your throat
is like the Tower of David, built
tall and sporting one thousand
shields, the weaponry of mighty
warriors. Your two breasts are two
fauns, a doe's twins pasturing in
roses. But before the day is gone and
the shadows disappear, I shall be off

to the myrrh-covered mountains and
the Lebanon foothills. You are so
beautiful, my darling, come with me
to the Lebanon to gaze, my bride,
down from the peak of Amana, from
the heights of Senir and Hermon,
the lairs of lions and mountain
leopards. My kindred bride, you
enrapture me with one blink of
the eye, with one curl round your
neck. How wonderful is your love, my
kindred bride, stronger than wine,
and a whiff of your scent
surpassing all spices. My bride,
your lips are moist with honey, your tongue
is honey and milk, and the aroma of
your dress has the scent of the
Lebanon. A private garden is my
kindred bride, a padlocked park,
a sealed-off spring well. Your limbs
are those of a pomegranate tree
with choice fruit, luscious and
spicy, with nard and saffron,
calamus, cinnamon, the sweet smelling
arbors, myrrh, aloe and frankincense,
together with the garden's brook,
its fresh-water well, and the run-off
of the Lebanon.

The Song of Songs of Solomon | 33

Rise up you Northwind, come now
you Southwind, blow through my
garden and spread its incense, so
that my love will come to his garden
and eat of its delectable fruit,

Chapter Five

I have come to my garden, my kindred
bride, having gotten my myrrh and
frankincense, having eaten my
honeycomb and its honey, having
downed my wine and milk, and having
dined with friends, drinking to
drunkenness.

I am asleep but my heart awakes,
my love knocks:

Open for me, my fiancée, my lovebird.
My head is moist with dew, my locks
with the night's dampness.

But I have taken off my clothes –
how can I redress? I have bathed
my feet – how can I soil them again?

Then my love pushed his hand through
the hole, while my whole body trembled
for him. I rose to open for my love,
with my hand and fingers sweating
sweet scent at the door handle.
I opened for my love but my love
had slipped away. My heart died
over this response of his. I sought
him but found him not; I called to
him but he answered not. The guards
who patrol the city discovered me and
they beat and hurt me. They stripped
off my veil, those guardians of
the ramparts.

"O daughters of Jerusalem, I adjure you
that if you find my love, what
shall you tell him – that I am lovesick."

"O lovely lady, why would your love
be any better that other loves, that
you adjure us so?"

"My love is bright and ruddy and
much decorated. His head like
bright gold, his bushy hair black
like a raven's. His eyes like doves
at the drinking trough, clear as

milk and placed just right. His cheeks
are patches of rare spices, his lips
roses moistened with crushed myrrh.
His hands clasps of gold, spangled
with gems, his chest a stand of
ivory embellished with sapphires.
His thighs pillars of marble set
in a golden housing. He looks
like the Lebanon with its vivacious
cedars. His mouth is delicious and
altogether wonderful. This is my
beloved companion, daughters of
Jerusalem."

Chapter Six

"Then where is your love, most
beautiful woman, where is your love
off to, so that we can search for
him with you?"

My love went off to his garden
with its furrows of spice, and to
pasture at the parkland, and to
collect roses. I am my love's and
he is mine, out there pasturing
amid the rosebushes.

My beloved, you are as lovely as
Tirza, striking as Jerusalem, and
breathtaking as a military parade.
Turn your eyes away from me, because they
overwhelm me. Those curls are
like a flock of billy goats descending
from Mount Gilead. Your teeth are
a family of sheep emerging from
the river, perfectly paired and
spotless. Your brow is like a
section of pomegranate seen from
behind your tresses. Of queens
there may be sixty, of wives eighty,
and countless maidens. But of my
exquisite dove there is only one,
unique to her mother, and whom
the maidens see and praise, whom the
queens and wives worship.

Who comes now, attractive as
dawn, bright as the moon, radiant
as the sun, dramatic as a march?
I had been at the walnut grove to
check on the sprouts at the riverbed,
to see if the grapes were ripening,
if the pomegranates were in bloom,
and I had not realized how soul-struck
I had become with the manifest
destiny of my noble people.

Chapter Seven

O lady of Shulam, come back here
so that we can look at you.

"Why peer at this Shulamith as if
she were in Mahanaim's dance fete?"

How gracious are your steps in those
slippers, noble lady! Your waist is
curved to an artist's ideal.
Your hips are moon-lite jugs filled to
the brim. Your belly is like a
bundle of grain belted with roses.
Your two breasts like two fauns,
the doe's twins. Your neck is like
a pillar of ivory, your eyes measured
pools at the capital gate. Your
nose like the Lebanon overlook, facing
Damascus. Your head placed like
the Carmel, with your hair entangling
a monarch in its silken strands.
How beautiful and wonderful is
this love and delight! Stately as
a palm tree, I would want to climb
this palm and take hold of its limbs,
to have your breasts be grape-clusters
and your breath apples. Your palate

is vintage wine, right for friendly
company and praised by sleepy drunks.

I belong to my love and my love loves
me. So come my love, let us go to
the country, we'll sleep in the hamlets
and wake at the vineyards to see if
the vines are in bloom, if the grapes
are ripening, if the pomegranates
are ready. It is there that I shall
present you with my love. The mandrakes
have released their aroma and we have
fresh produce at the door, together
with your regular favorites which I
have been keeping for you.

Chapter Eight

I wish you were my brother, having
suckled with me at mother's breasts.
I could then meet you in the street
and kiss you, and nobody would be
mean to me. I would lead you to mother's
house, where you would be in charge,
and I would pour you vintage wines
and pomegranate nectar – with the
left hand under my head and the right hand hugging me.

"O daughters of Jerusalem, swear to
me that you will not rouse or spur
this passion until its time."

"Who is this coming out of the desert
and holding on to her companion?"

I once did excite you under the
apple tree, where your own mother
gave birth to you, where your mother
had conceived you. Engrave me onto
your heart and seal me on your arm,
for love is strong as death, and jealousy
is terrible as the tomb, her flame
burning like a sparkling fire. Steady
downpours cannot extinguish love and
rivers cannot douse her. Should someone
offer to buy off love with all his wealth,
he would be rejected angrily. Now, we have
a little sister who has no breasts yet. What shall
we do for our sister when they discuss her
prospects? If she were a wall we could build her
up with a silver balcony, and if she were a door,
we could enhance her with a cedar plank. I am
a wall and my breasts rise like towers, so that I
find favor in his eyes.

Solomon owned a vineyard at the population center, and he turned the vineyard over to sharecroppers, each to earn a thousand shekels at harvest time.

> Solomon, I have my own vineyard, and
> I shall give the thousand to you,
> and even give the sharecroppers
> two hundred.

> You, there in the vineyard, sing
> forth, for I and my friends want to
> hear your voice.

> Then run along, my love, to be
> like a stag or young gazelle on
> spice-covered mountains.

* * *

Recommended reading:
HAROLD FISCH, "The Song of Solomon: The Allegorical Imperative," in *Poetry with a Purpose*, 1990.

The Book of Lamentations

OW COULD A great metropolis turn empty, widow-like, or a world power turn into a puppet state? There is crying through the night, tears wetting the cheeks with no friend to console, all allies being liars and becoming antagonists. It is the Jewish State which has been driven into exile, in poverty and hard labor, among nations which offer no asylum, where her pursuers force her to the wall.

Jerusalem recalls the delight of the good old days during these days of her calamity, when her populace fell to attackers, with no defenders and the enemy laughing at her defeat. It is because of Jerusalem's sins she has become an outcast; those who once respected her now poke fun, and she herself sighs and sits at the back. Her ugliness was revealed in a way she had not imagined and she now has dropped into helplessness – O Lord, see my despair, for the enemy rules. Enemies have taken over everything sacred, occupying the temple, where You commanded they not enter.

The people mutter as they search for food, having pawned

their jewels to keep alive. O Lord, see how I have become a glutton.

I would not wish this on anybody anywhere. One shall not find a tragedy great as my tragedy, which God contrived in His anger. He flashed lightning from on high to singe me and placed a trap at my feet to bring me down, confusing me with constant consternation. Clamping the burden of my misdeeds onto my neck to break me, the Lord gave me an unbearable load. The Lord has cut down my soldiery, has set the stage for undoing my young men and for squeezing the blood out of Judah's virgin girls. Consolation is beyond me and my eyes cry bitter tears while mighty powers devastate my sons.

Zion has thrown up her hands and is beyond consolation, because the Lord has ordered that Jacob be surrounded by foes, with Jerusalem demonized among them. The Lord is justified because I have disobeyed Him. O all nations, hear and witness my punishment, as my men and women go into captivity. I called to my allies but they misled me, and now my elderly are dying in the streets where they search for food to survive.

O Lord, see how bitter is my disobedience, my stomach churning and my heart melting, because outside there is the murderous sword and inside is the house of death. When the enemy hears my uncontrollable moans they rejoice over my loss. But O Lord, all this is Your doing, so set a date for their judgment, for them to become like me. Add up their abundant evils and do to them what You have done to me due to my many sins, for which my desperate heart aches.

Chapter Two

How could God besmirch Zion, tossing Israel's heavenly glory to the ground and, in His anger, being unmindful of His little niche! Mercilessly, He ravaged Jacob's territories, angrily pulverizing Judah's bulwark, decimating the monarchy and its princes. In rage, He crushed Israel's defenses, interfered with the armed resistance, and set flaming fires ablaze all around. He bent a bow like an archer, His armory prepared for attack, in order to slaughter whoever is comely in Zion's habitat, pouring out conflagration with hate.

Yes, God played the enemy in Israel's destruction, destroying her mansions and embankments, and there planting shrieks and groans. He mowed down the tabernacle like grass and befouled His temple. He cancelled Zion's Sabbaths and Festivals, and defiled both monarch and priest. The Lord abandoned His altar, closed His sanctuary, and assigned foreigners to the halls and precincts, where they raise a shout in celebration.

God carefully planned this ruining of Zion's ramparts. He measured them precisely, then tore down both wall and militia totally. Her gates crumbled, her bolts smashed, He sent both king and prince out to the uncivilized world, with her prophets bereft of visions from God. The elders of Zion sit on the dusty ground in silence wearing sackcloth, while Jerusalem's maidens lower their heads.

Blinded by tears, my stomach gurgles and my gall spills to the ground, all because my people are in collapse, with infants gasping in the city streets. They call to their mothers for food and drink, writhing near death, then pouring out their souls at their mother's bosom.

O men of Jerusalem, O daughters of Zion, what testimony, what parallel, what comparison can I offer to console you when your downfall is as deep as the ocean, beyond repair. Your visionaries projected worthless pictures for you. Instead of telling you to repent of your sins, they conjured up meaningless distractions. Now all passers-by clasp their hands, whistle, and shake their heads over Jerusalem, to ask: Could this be the city they once called the embodiment of beauty, the toast of the planet? Opponents pour out derision, whistling while gnashing their teeth, to say: We conquered; the day we long hoped for we are witnessing. But it was the Lord who carried out this happening, actualizing His pronouncement from early on, condemning without compassion, letting the foe rejoice in triumph.

O you walls of Zion, shed rivers of tears, give your eyes no rest neither by day nor night. Rise up to wail during the nights, pouring out your heart's torrents before God. Raise hands toward Him on behalf of the children who are starving to death in the public squares.

O Lord, look and consider to whom You have done these things: To have mothers eat their suckling babes, to have priests and prophets murdered in the temple. Everywhere, both boys and seniors squat in the dirt, both maidens and men perish by the sword, because You have proceeded wantonly on Your day of vengeance. You proclaimed a celebration for the states that surround us. There were no survivors during God's day of anger, as the enemy snuffed out the souls which I nurtured and raised.

Chapter Three

א

I am the man who witnessed a holocaust devised by His anger.
It is I He thrust into this blackness without light,
Only to strike me with repeated blows at the dawn.

ב

He wore out my body, from skin to bones,
Then constructed high barricades and moats around me,
To place me in the terminal darkness of death:

ג

There to imprison me under heavy chains,
And when I shouted and begged, He cut off my prayers.
He put me in a steel block to impede escape:

ד

Outside were bears and vicious lions hidden in lairs,
And thorn-lined obstructions to render me hopeless.
He used me as the target for His archery:

ה

Striking my backside with arrows, for laughs,
With a crowd howling around me all day long,
He stuffed me with bitters and fed me poison:

ו

He chipped my teeth using cinders and made me bite the dust.
I am beyond longing for peace and for the good life,
And I view my survival as beyond even God:

ז

O, think of my despair which is meaner than hemlock,
Remember me and heal my fractured soul.
Yet, I tell myself that there is hope:

ח

Because God's kindness is sure, with mercies unending,
Reappearing each morning in steadfast faithfulness,
My soul says stand by the Lord and trust in Him:

ט

God is good to those who trust Him, the souls that seek Him.
It is good to be still and await God's help,
It is good for the individual to face struggles at first:

י

Let him remain quiet while bearing his burden,
Let him swallow his complaint out of a glimmer of hope,
Let him offer a cheek to his attacker, accepting the shame:

כ

Of course the Lord does not punish forever,
When ready, He turns merciful to spread His goodness,
For He has no pleasure in tormenting humanity:

ל

To crush underfoot each inhabitant on earth,
To commit an injustice in sight of the heavens,
To wrong a litigant, as if God does not see:

מ

And who can command and create if God objects?

For it is not God who creates evil with the good.

So let people not complain after they go sinning:

ג

Instead we should examine our actions and return to the Lord.

Let us turn our hearts up toward the Lord in heaven.

True, we have transgressed – but do You forgive?

ס

You draped yourself in rage and pursued us relentlessly,

You hid in the clouds, closing off our prayers,

You cast us out to scorn among the nations:

פ

Our enemies spew steady curses upon us,

We have trepidation, entrapment, expulsion and defeat.

Now I cry streams of tears over our catastrophe:

ע

I shall never desist, nor dry my moist eyes

Until the Lord up in heaven looks here to take note,

Because I was touched more than anyone by what happened:

צ

My rivals trapped me like a bird for no reason,

They dumped me in a pit, then threw down stones,

They dunked me in deep water, I almost died:

ק

I called out God's name from the depths:

Hear my voice, do not reject this supplication,

Be accepting as I approach, say: Fear not:

ר

O Lord, rise up for the rescue of my life, my soul.
O Lord, You have seen their wrongs, so get me justice,
You have witnessed their premeditated vengeance:

ש

You are aware of their campaign of defamation,
Their gossip and daily scheming against me,
With an agenda that harps only on me from start to finish:

ת

O Lord, repay them fully in kind, with interest,
Damn them with an irreversible heart condition,
Drive them out in fury beyond Your heavenly skies.

Chapter Four

WOULD GOLD TARNISH or bullion decay or sacred dia-
mond be thrown away in the street! Then how could
the precious children of Zion – dear as gold – be treated like
mere earthenware, a potter's product? Even a hyena mother ex-
tends a breast to suckle her cub, but my nation's mothers have
turned cold, like desert vultures. A newborn's tongue clings
to his cheek from thirst and a baby cries for food, but no one
offers. They had been fed royally but now are starving in the
streets. They had dressed up in silks but now pick from garbage
dumps. All this due to my people's sins, which surpass the sins
of even Sodom, when it was destroyed of a sudden.

Our white-haired holy men, clean as snow and whose bright

bodies were ruddy as sapphire, now have turned into coal-dirt figures, with wooden skin clinging to the bone. The luckier men died by the sword – instead of hunger – their blood spilled at once while they were still well fed. Gentle women now cook up their children for a meal, during this national tragedy.

It is the Lord unleashing His pent-up anger, pouring His fiery rage onto Zion, burning it to the ground. From monarch to citizen, no one anywhere believed that an enemy attack could penetrate the gates of Jerusalem.

It has happened because of the conduct of her prophets and priests, as they presided over the spilling of innocent blood. They strode through the streets seeing nothing, thus sullied by the blood of victims, as if wearing blood-stained clothes. Call after them, "Keep away, they are dirty, they contaminate." Even in exile, tell the Gentiles not to let them stay. God scattered them because He did not want to look at them anymore, after they dishonored the priesthood and disrespected the elders.

We are moaning after having banked on a worthless trust, counting on allies who would not help. Now we are fearful of walking through our own streets, and our end is in sight, for we are finished.

Our pursuers were swifter than eagles. They attacked us on the mountains, they raided us in the deserts. Our lifelong leader, God's designate – under whose protection we had hoped to survive in the exile – was captured in their foray.

O, you people of Edom, rejoice and celebrate there in your land of Uz, until you too will be handed the cup of hemlock, for you to swallow and throw up. O, people of Zion, your punishment is now complete, you shall be exiled no more. People of Edom, your incrimination is upcoming, with your glaring evils to be made public.

Chapter Five

O LORD, BE REMINDED of what happened to us, look and see our degradation. Our country was occupied by foreigners and our homes housed strangers. We became like fatherless orphans, our mothers like widows. We had to pay for our own drinking water and firewood. We were up to our necks in work and were given no respite.

We had trade agreements with Egypt and Assyria for our basic food. Our fathers made these worthless pacts, but soon died and left us to suffer the consequences.

Lowlifes came to rule over us with a heavy hand. We earned our keep in constant danger of raids from the desert. Our flesh turned fiery red from hunger. Zion's matrons and maidens were ravished in the midst of Judea's cities. Our officials were hanged by their hands, over the pleas from our elders. Young men were forced to carry shale and adolescents had to chop wood. No longer were there consultations with the elderly at city gates, and the young folks had no music. There was no more joy in living, as dancing had turned to mourning.

Because of our sinning, the nation's pride and joy was destroyed. While all other things were terrible, it is this thing that makes our hearts ache most: To see Mount Zion in ruin, with foxes ambling through —.

O Lord, Your majesty is eternal and Your rule is unending. But please do not overlook us forever, to abandon us for such a long time. O Lord, beckon us back to You and we shall return repentant. Bring back the good old days for us. You have raged against us more than enough, for You punished us exceedingly.

The Book of Ruth

I T HAPPENED THAT during the reign of the Judges there was a famine in the land, so that a certain man in Judea left Bethlehem to live in the plains of Moab, he with his wife and two sons. The man's name Elimelech, his wife's name Naomi, his two sons Mahlon and Chilion, each one prominent in Bethlehem and Judea. They moved to the plains of Moab and settled there. Then Naomi's husband Elimelech died and she was left with her two sons. They married Moabite women, one named Orpah, the second Ruth, and all of them lived there for about ten years. Then Mahlon and Chilion too died, so that Naomi was left bereft of her sons and her husband.

Taking her daughters-in-law, Naomi prepared to return from the plains of Moab, for she had heard, there in the plains of Moab, that the Lord had remembered His own people and given them bread. Leaving the place in order to return to the land of Judea, she set off on the road with her two daughters-in-law.

Then Naomi said to them, "Stay, go on to your own mother's place. May the Lord be kind to you, for you were kind to the deceased and to me; may the Lord grant you contentment, each in her husband's home." She gave them farewell kisses, and all cried bitterly. "No, we will come with you to your people," they answered. Naomi repeated, "Stay, my dear girls, why should you come with me? Are there boys in my womb that could marry you? Leave me, dear girls, for I am too old to marry. Even if I mustered some hope for myself, and spent this very night with a man and gave birth to sons, should you wait for them to grow up, tying yourselves down for them, not marrying? No, my dear girls, and see how it is even worse for me because I am being punished by God." They all cried some more, wailing. Orpah then kissed her mother-in-law goodbye, but Ruth clung to her.

"See, your sister-in-law is returning to her people and her gods, return with her," Naomi said. Said Ruth, "Don't press me to leave, to abandon you, for where you go I shall go, and when you rest I shall rest, your people are my people and your God my God, and where you die I will die, to be buried there – I swear to God that death alone shall part me from you." Seeing how insistent she was on accompanying her, Naomi said nothing more.

They went on together until they reached Bethlehem. When they entered Bethlehem the entire city buzzed, the women exclaiming, "Can this be Naomi?" She answered, "Don't call me the nice Naomi, call me the mean Marra, because God has embittered me. I left here brimful and God brings me back impoverished, so don't call me the nice Naomi, for the Almighty has testified and punished me."

Such was Naomi's homecoming, accompanied by her daughter-in-law, Ruth the Moabite coming from the plains of Moab, and when they reached Bethlehem it was at the start of the barley harvest.

Chapter Two

THERE WAS A relative of Naomi's husband – a great gentleman in Elimelech's family – whose name was Boaz. Meanwhile, Ruth the Moabite told Naomi, "Let me go to the fields to pick up grain, wherever they are kind to me." "Go, my child," said Naomi. She went to collect grains after the reapers and she happened upon the field of Boaz, Elimelech's relative. Just then Boaz was arriving from Bethlehem, greeting the field hands with "God be with you," and they answered "God bless you." Boaz then asked his foreman, "Whose is this girl?" The foreman responded as follows: "She is a Moabite girl who returned with Naomi from the plains of Moab. She asked to pick up after the harvesters and she went working from morning 'til now and just for the moment she is resting inside a bit."

"You heard him my girl," said Boaz to Ruth, "so don't go gathering in any other field, neither leave this one but stay here with my maids. Find out which plot they will be harvesting next and follow them – I'm ordering the workers not to bother you. If you get thirsty, go to the jugs for the water that the workers draw." Her face fell and she bowed low, saying to him, "Why are you so kind to recognize me when I am but a foreigner?" Boaz explained, "I heard of what you did for your mother-in-law after your husband's death, how you left your father and mother and your native land to venture to a nation you never knew. May God reward your deed and be you paid in full by the Lord, God of Israel, under whose wing you have placed your trust." She said, "Sir, I your maidservant have found favor in your eyes, for you have touched my heart and consoled me, while I am less worthy than your maidservants."

At lunchtime, Boaz said to her, "Come there, have something, and dip your bread in the bitters." She sat beside the field hands with the toasted kernels that he offered her, eating her fill and more. Then she went back to gathering, while Boaz told his workers, "Let her gather even between the sheaves, don't abuse her, and leave her some stalks, and don't yell at her." She gathered in the field 'til evening, and when she threshed what she had collected it came to a bushelful of barley. This she carried to the city and showed her mother-in-law, presenting her with what was left from her lunch. Her mother-in-law exclaimed, "Where did you gather today – may your benefactor be blessed!" Then she told her mother-in-law that the name of the person where she labored all day was Boaz. "God bless him for his unceasing kindness for the living and the dead. This man is our relative, a next-of-kin," she told her. Then Ruth the Moabite added, "He even told me to befriend his young men, through to the end of the harvest." But Naomi said to her daughter-in-law Ruth, "It is all right for you to go out with his girls, and you are not to find yourself in any other field." So she kept company with Boaz's maids to the end of the barley and wheat harvests, all the while living with her mother-in-law.

Chapter Three

THEN HER MOTHER-IN-LAW Naomi addressed her as follows: "My dear daughter, certainly we must arrange for you to settle down properly. Now our relation Boaz, with whose maids you've kept company, is winnowing his storehouse of barley tonight. Bathe, put on makeup, dress up and go down to the storehouse, but don't let him see you while he finishes his food and drink. When he goes to sleep – find out where he sleeps – uncover the foot of his resting place and lie down. Then he will tell you what to do." "I do whatever you tell me," she answered.

She went down to the silo, doing everything her mother-in-law said. Boaz ate, drank, was merry, and went to sleep at the edge of the barley heap. She came quietly, uncovered his feet and stretched out. In the middle of the night the man stirred and was shocked to find a woman sleeping at this feet, and asked, "Who are you?" She said, "I am your maidservant Ruth, here for you to spread your wings over your maidservant, since you are a kinsman." "May the Lord bless you, my dear," he said, "and this present kindness for your mother-in-law is even greater than your first one, in that you are not running off with one of the young men, whether rich or poor. Not to worry, I will do whatever you say, for all my neighbors know how you are a worthy woman. But while it is true that I am a next-of-kin, there is a next-of-kin who is closer than I. Stay the night, and in the morning if he redeems you, fine; and if he refuses, I swear to God that I will redeem. Sleep 'til morning."

She slept at his feet until morning and got up before anyone could see, because he did not want it known that a woman had been at the silo. He said, "Hand me the shawl you have on." He took hold of it and measured out six measures of barley, placing it on her to take back to the city.

She returned to her mother-in-law, who said, "How did you do, my child?" and she related what the man was doing for her and added, "These six barley measures did he give me, saying he did not want me to come to you empty-handed." "Sit tight, my child," said Naomi, "until you hear how the matter goes, because the man will not rest until he deals with it this very day."

Boaz went to the city gate and established himself there. The next-of-kin mentioned by Boaz was passing by and Boaz called out, "Come sit here, buddy." He came over and sat down. Next, Boaz assembled ten of the city elders and asked them to sit down; they sat down. Boaz then addressed the next-of-kin: "The plot of land that belonged to our brother Elimelech was sold by Naomi who now returned from the plains of Moab. I thought to advise you to commit yourself in front of those sitting here and the nation's elders. If you intend to redeem, redeem it; otherwise inform me, because you are the principal redeemer and I come after you." "I shall redeem," he responded. Then Boaz went on: "On the day you acquire the land at the behest of

Naomi and Ruth the Moabite, this Ruth the Moabite, erstwhile wife of the deceased, are you to take so as to memorialize the deceased via his inheritance." The next-of-kin then said, "Then I cannot redeem, lest I impugn my own inheritance. You go ahead and redeem my redemption, for I cannot redeem."

It was once the tradition in Israel when formalizing a redemption, an exchange, or any agreement, that a person would remove his shoe and hand it to his partner, this being the Israelite practice. So the redeemer said to Boaz, "Here take it," and he removed his shoe.

Then Boaz declared before the elders and the assembled: "You witness that today I do acquire all that belonged to Elimelech and to Chilion and Mahlon which is under Naomi's charge. Further, that I do take Ruth the Moabite, erstwhile wife of Mahlon, in marriage, to memorialize the departed via his inheritance, so that the dear departed not be forgotten by his brethren and his locality. You all are witnesses this day."

"Witnessed!" proclaimed those at the gate and the elders, "God grant that this woman who enters your home be like Rachel and Leah who between them created the House of Israel, and that you do great things in Ephrath and become famous in Bethlehem. May your home become like the home of Perez – Judah's son by Tamar – by the offspring that God grants you with this young woman."

Boaz took Ruth in marriage, he husbanded her, God granted her a pregnancy, and she bore a son. The women said to Naomi, "Blessed be God who did not deny you a kinsman this day. May he be known throughout Israel and be your joy and provider in your old age, for he is the child of your beloved daughter-in-law who is more precious to you than any seven sons."

Naomi took charge of the child, set it on her lap and raised it, so that the women quipped, "A son is born to Naomi." They named him Obed, and he became the father of Jesse, the father of David.

The Perez lineage is as follows: Perez fathered Hezron, Hezron fathered Rom, Rom had Amminadab, Amminadab had Nahshon, Nachshon had Salmah. Then Salmon had Boaz, and Boaz had Obed, and Obed had Jesse, and Jesse had David.

Understanding the Personifications in
The Book of Proverbs

THE PROVERBS OF Solomon, son of David, King of Israel. For the appreciation of wisdom and morality, and for the recognition of thought-out ideas. Toward the acceptance of ethical absolutes, namely Righteousness, Justice, and Honesty. Offering insight for the simpleton, knowledge and know-how for the young. Let the wise man listen so as to broaden his learning, and so the thinker may become brilliant. All these through an understanding of the proverb and its idiom, through the expressions of learned men.

Knowledge begins with the reverence of the Lord; thus evildoers reject wisdom and civility.

My son, listen to your father's advice and do not neglect your mother's teaching. These will place grace 'round your head and a garland about your neck.

Greed personified

Son, if sins tempt you, say no. When they say, "Come with us, we shall kill those innocents. We will send the live ones to their grave, the unsuspecting off to hell. All the booty we accrue shall fill our homes with riches. Your lot will be in with ours, we shall all share one purse." Son, do not join them. Avoid their ways because they run toward troubles ending quickly in death. Just as birds are unaware of hidden snares stretched out to trap and kill them, just so is the person who is motivated by greed. It captures his soul.

Wisdom personified
Wisdom sings forth, making herself heard in the streets, facing the crowd at the village gate, her announcement resounding all through town: "How long will you simpletons adore superficiality, and you jokers love jokes, and you fools despise reason! Turn to my admonitions so that I can impart my spirit; let me teach you my ways. But because I called and you refused me, I extended a hand and you did not take notice. You contradict my suggestions and refuse my advice. I, for my part, will laugh at your troubles, will mock you when terror strikes, when terror comes in like a storm and troubles like a hurricane, when you are overcome by despair and disaster. Then will you call for me and I shall not answer, you will seek and not find me. All this because you despise learning and choose not to fear the Lord. Thus, they did not follow my advice. They scorned my admonitions, so let them swallow the bitter fruit of their ways and become stuffed with their schemes. Let the simpleton's dullness kill him and the fool's paradise finish him. Whereas those who obey me can rest assured, safe from fear of evil."

Chapter Two

M Y SON, ACCEPT what I say and keep my commands, bend an ear to wisdom and turn your heart toward knowledge, call out to learning and raise your voice for understanding, seek it like silver and like a treasure trove. Only then will you know the reverence due to God and attain knowledge of the Divine. For it is God who grants wisdom, He is the source of knowledge and understanding. It is He who grants salvation to the just, protecting those who proceed honestly and preserving the ways of Justice – the approach which His devotees sustain. You too can comprehend righteousness and justice, simple honesty and doing the right thing.

When wisdom fills your heart and your soul tastes learning, your discretion can protect and preserve you. It will keep you from evil, from a man who spews lies, from all those who abandon simple truth to walk in the dark, from those who enjoy doing wrong, rejoicing in their evil contrariness and crookedness, having lost their way entirely.

Idolatry personified

It will keep you from an alien woman, a pagan with smooth speech who abandons her youthful Master and denies the covenant with Divinity. Her place leads down to hell, killing anyone who visits. Those who approach her can never escape to find their way to life. Instead, son, walk the good walk, keeping to the pious path. Because it is the good and simple folk who will fill the globe, while criminals and liars shall perish from the earth.

Chapter Three

S ON, DON'T FORGET what I am teaching you, take my commandments to heart. They will secure for you a long and peaceful life. Hold onto kindliness and truth, clasping them to your chest and engraving them onto your heart. Then will you achieve popularity and acceptance in the eyes of God and man:

Trust God with all your heart and don't rely on your wit.

Turn to God in whatever you do, and He will grant you smooth sailing.

Don't think you are so smart, but remember God to avoid evil. Thereby will you have nourishment for your belly and marrow for your bones.

Honor God with both your riches and first fruits. Thereby will your barns fill with grain and your reservoirs with wine.

Son, do not recoil from my lessoning and rebuke. For the Creator rebukes those He loves, the same way that a father treats his son.

Fortunate is the person who adopts Wisdom. She is more profitable and productive than silver or gold. She is more precious than gems or anything you own. With her right hand she offers long life and with her left hand wealth and honor. She proceeds along the byways of courtesy and peace. She is the tree of life and happiness for her devotees.

God himself drafted wisdom to create the universe, setting up the heavens through science. His thinking sank the seas and made the skies drip dew. Therefore, my son, do not lose sight of wisdom and understanding, these providing spirit for your soul and grace 'round your throat. Then may you progress securely and not stumble. You will rest having pleasant sleep, without fears. You will not fear sudden dangers nor attack by antagonists. God shall be your safety net to protect you from entrapment:

Do not withhold a favor from a deserving friend when it is within your power to grant it.

Do not tell your friend: I will give it to you if you come back tomorrow – when you have it right there.

Do not scheme against a friend who trusts you.

Do not envy the strong-arm man, neither follow his lead. For God hates the crook, but He communes with men of honor. God's curses fill the evildoer's house, whereas God blesses the dwelling of the righteous. Against scorners He plays games, but for the humble He provides grace. Honor goes to the wise, while fools collect shame.

Chapter Four

Tradition personified

C HILDREN, LISTEN TO your father's lesson with instructions on how to become wise. I have good material, so do not abandon my teachings. For I too was a son to a father, and an only child to my mother. They taught me saying: Let my words enrich your heart, observe my directives for life. Acquire wisdom, acquire understanding – don't forget or fudge what I tell you. It can sustain you. Wisdom begins when you shop for wisdom. With whatever else you collect get brain power. Nurture it and it will elevate you; hold it and it will bring you respect. It will place grace atop your head, to cap you with an aura of beauty.

So my son, accept my vision and you will gain many years of life. Teaching you the ways of wisdom points you down a straight path so that you can proceed without worry, even speed along merrily. Now hold fast to this warning as your life depends on it: Do not follow in the pathways of crooks, to move along their evil ways. Reject them, do not enter, leave them behind. They do not rest until they do something evil, and lose sleep when they cannot wrong someone. Their very foods derive from wrongdoing, their drinks from violence. But the road of the righteous is like a bright sunrise, which will continue to shine at high noon. But the road of the evildoer is dark with hidden pitfalls.

So son, hear these pronouncements and bend your ear to my words. Don't overlook them but keep them in your heart. They are life-giving to their possessor and medicine for the whole body. And most importantly protect your heart, because it controls one's way of life. Avoid foul language and keep lies from your lips. Look straight ahead, eyeing a worthwhile objective. Set out honestly and your entire adventure will succeed. Turn not right or left, avoid that step toward evil.

Chapter Five

Idolatry vs. Faith personified

M Y SON, LISTEN to wisdom. Bend an ear to my knowledge so that you will have insight and become aware of the power of speech. Here, this alien lady spouts with her honey-sweet lips, with her slippery tongue. But in the end she becomes a bitter pill and as sharp as a two-edged sword. Her feet lead to death, her steps head toward hell. Lest you misjudge the approach to life and not realize how devious is her purpose. So children, listen to me and don't slink away from this warning: Stay away from her and even do not go near her house. Lest there you will be giving away your glory to others, your years to ruffians. Lest a stranger sap your strength and your fortune fill a stranger's home. In the end, you would be groaning with your flesh and frame near collapse, saying: "How could I have despised wisdom by rejecting your admonition! I did not obey my teacher, bending no ear to instructions. I almost personified evil amidst the congregation and the public." Instead, satisfy your thirst with your own well water which flows from your private sources. Your own spring well overflows all around, with torrents through the streets. Yours is a blessed heritage, so rejoice as with a childhood sweetheart. She is like a loving doe who presents beautifully, with breasts to quench your thirst at all times and to thrill you with her passion. So son, why turn passionate with a stranger and hug an alien bosom? For God watches the ways of men, monitoring their progress. An evildoer becomes trapped by his own misdeeds, hanged by the strands of his sins. His death results from dismissing warnings and from a multitude of wrongs.

Chapter Six

S ON, IF YOU gave a fellow your guarantee, having committed yourself to a businessman, but now you have become trapped through this agreement which you made. Alas son, do this to save yourself, by accepting that the other fellow has control over you. Lower yourself and offer to give the fellow whatever is his by right. Do not close your eyes nor sleep on it. Save yourself at once, like a deer or dove from a snare.

Lethargic one, go visit an ant to learn wisdom from her ways. She has no manager, officer or boss but she prepares her food during summertime, anticipating her requirements starting at harvest.

Lazy one, how long will you rest to finally get out of bed? By a little more sleep, a few more winks, some more lazyboning in bed, you may end up as poor as when accosted by an armed robber.

The criminal-type mischief-maker operates by mouthing lies. He winks with his eyes, taps with his feet, and points with his fingers. But he harbors propaganda, cultivating repeated evils and fomenting disputes. His downfall comes suddenly and he will not survive the crash.

The Lord hates the following six, and especially the seventh: Haughty eyes; a lying tongue; murderous hands; a scheming heart; fleeting feet for mischief; a false witness; and those who foment disputes between neighbors.

My son, keep your father's commandments and do not neglect your mother's teachings. Wrap them about your heart always, bind them to your throat. They will guide you when you go out, guard you when you sleep, and instruct you when you wake. For the Commandment is like a candle, and the Torah is like its light, but it is the chastisement of rebuke which provides a direction for living. It protects you from an evil woman, an alien's smooth talk. Lest you lust after her for her beauty, as she seduces you with good looks. But the chasing after harlots can turn a man into a slob, and even a precious soul may lose himself over another man's wife. Can a man nurse a fire on his lap and not burn his clothing? Can a man walk on hot embers and not burn his feet? Just so, whoever approaches a neighbor's wife cannot escape unharmed. Because people will not despise a thief who steals, perhaps so as to feed his hungry soul. When caught, he can pay back, even seven times over and giving everything in the house. But the man who commits adultery is deranged – only a maniac would do it. For his punishment and shame will never finish. Since the husband's anger is fueled by jealousy he will show no mercy at the time of retribution. He will not be bribed, no matter how much is offered.

Chapter Seven

Idolatry/Atheism personified

S ON, REMEMBER MY instructions, hold them tight. Observe my commands for life. Shield them like the apple of your eye, bracelet them at your fingers, and inscribe them on your heart. Consider wisdom your sister and knowledge your own mate. This will protect you from a strange woman, the alien with tricky words. Because I looked out of a side window and spotted a simple, uncouth lad. He left the market and went to an alley toward her house, in the gloom as nighttime darkness was creeping in. There stood the woman, strong willed and dressed like a prostitute. She is loud, provocative and does not stay in. Sometimes in the yard, sometimes in the street, she lurks at every corner. She takes hold of the lad with a kiss and says brazenly: "I owed sacrificial offerings and today I finally made good on my pledge. This is why I came looking for you and I found you. I put fresh bedding on my couch, with Egyptian linen tapestry, and perfumed with myrrh, aloe and cinnamon. Come let us embrace in the delight of love 'til morning. The Mister is not home, is on a long journey. He took the bag of silver with him, and is to return at some unknown date." Her long, slick speech persuades him, and he swiftly follows her – like an ox trotting to the slaughter and like a bird flying into its trap. As a snake strikes the unaware, a would-be arrow punctures his liver. So children, listen to what I say: Do not give mind to her crooked ways, for she has already slain a multitude, with the corpses mere bones now. Her dwelling leads to the cemetery, to a place of death.

Chapter Eight

Wisdom vs. Folly personified

WISE WISDOM CALLS forth as well. Standing on heights, along roads, in residential neighborhoods, at city gates, there where people enter, she raises her voice: Humanity, I call forth, so that the foolish ones may grow in knowledge and understanding. Listen up, because I bring an important and sound message. I tell the truth, for my lips abhor wrong. I speak for righteousness, avoiding any tricks, and presenting what is right and proper for men of understanding. Therefore, accept my thought-out wisdom as better than silver or gold. Wisdom is more precious than diamonds and nothing you own compares.

I am Wisdom. Having studied sagacity and mastered thought, I conclude that since reverence for the Lord means hating evil, I in turn hate pride, mischief and lips that lie. Further, I offer advice, solutions, insight, and power. It is through me that monarchs rule and senators legislate soundly. With me do officials function, and philanthropists contribute as expected. I love those who love me, and am at the service of those who seek me. Wealth and honor reside with me, for stable endowments and expenditures. My profits are higher than holdings of gold, bullion, or silver. I proceed from justice and the rule of law, so as to enrich my admirers by stuffing their warehouses full.

In the beginning God initiated me, even before He started His creation. I was appointed first in time, before the universe. I functioned before there were the massive waters of the deep and their hot springs. I was there before the mountains and plateaus rose up and before He fashioned the ground, plains and farmlands. I stood by when He readied the heavens and calculated the rotations across space, and when He fastened the sky above and tunneled the wellsprings below, and when He established the limits of the seas so that the waters would not flood unauthorized, and when he set the laws of nature for the globe. I became His apprentice, a daily delight, traipsing before Him at all times. I then danced over His worldwide property, and now I play with the people. So children, listen to me, and fortunate will be he who follows my ways. Accept this criticism, wise up, and don't be lackadaisical. Lucky is he who obeys me, always coming to my door, waiting daily at my doorposts, because whoever engages me engages life and wins the favor of God. But whoever antagonizes me hates himself – all enemies of mine love death.

Wisdom then builds a home, cementing its seven-fold foundation. She prepares food, pours out wine, and sets a table for dinner. She sends her maids uptown with an invitation, to announce as follows: "If you are a simpleton or boor come here. You will eat of my bread and drink of my wine and abandon your foolish ways. Rise to a life of reason.

If you rebuke a scorner, it is you who will be ashamed, and when you correct an evildoer, the error is yours.

Do not rebuke a scorner lest he despise you, but rebuke a wise man and he will love you.

Impart to the wise and he becomes wiser; advise the pious and he becomes learned.

Wisdom starts with the fear of the Lord, and sacred knowledge is the ultimate. "I can lengthen your days and add years to your life. When you turn wise, the gain is all yours, and if you fool around, you alone will suffer."

The woman of Folly, the foolish know-nothing, calls forth also. Seated at the door of her home, on a chair facing uptown, she calls to the passers-by who are going about their own business, to say: "If you are a simpleton or boor, come here. My stolen waters are sweeter and the unlawful loaf is most delicious." He does not realize that she harbors thugs, and that all her guests end deep in hell.

Chapters 9 through 23 feature mainly the one-verse proverbs which are adequately translated in several Hebrew Bibles. Toward the middle of chapter 23 the text returns to the longer, narrative forms of the Book's beginning.

Chapter Twenty-Three Verse Twenty-Six

MY SON, GIVE me your heart and let your eyes follow my ways. Thus, a harlot is a deep ditch and the strange wife is a faulty fountain. For suddenly she will be off hunting for the other adulterous men. Ouch, who has woes, conflicts, arguments, needless injuries, and bloody eyes? Those who drink late into the night and go on search for high-proof vintage. So don't inspect that wine for richness, eyeing it in the glass, and expect later to be walking in a straight line. It ends with poisoning you like a snakebite.

Then your sights will peer at harlots and your heart will

conjure up dreadful things. Imagine being out at sea swinging from the top mast, muttering: If you hit me I do not hurt, smack me I do not mind, and when I get sober I will find some more.

Chapter Twenty-Four

D O NOT BE envious of evil men and do not think to join them. There is violence in their hearts and they preach crime. Instead, plan on building your home with a solid foundation. Use intelligence to fully furnish its rooms richly. A wise person is firm, since intelligence gives you strength. Plan a strategy for conflicts, and success comes from sufficient advice.

Wisdom is beyond the capability of the lowlife, so he cannot open his mouth at a townhall meeting. His plans are for doing evil and will be tagged the master schemer. The lowlife's scheme is for sinning, while the joker plans for a travesty.

If you falter in face of danger you are indeed the weakling, standing back from saving those being slaughtered and those at the edge of the sword. Should you answer, "We did not know," but the Creator of all hearts will know and punish accordingly.

My son, eat up the sweet honey which is so delicious. Just so, absorb precious wisdom into your soul, for a future time, and there is always hope.

Do not introduce the evildoer into the dwelling of the righteous, not to disturb his homestead. For a righteous man can fall seven times and rise again, but evildoers crash with their evil.

Do not celebrate when your enemy falls. When he trips do not rejoice, lest the Lord take note to consider it wrong and withdraw His punishment from him. Do not compete with mischief-makers and be not envious of the lawless. For there is no future for evil, as the criminal's candle burns down. My son, fear God and the king, staying far from both breakaway types. Because their demise comes without warning, and no one knows just how.

These proverbs too are for the wise judges: Preferential treatment in justice makes for wrong. Whoever pronounces a criminal right, will be cursed roundly by the peoples and the nations. But anyone who reprimands will flourish and will reap avid blessings. Whoever answers appropriately wins kisses on his lips.

Make preparations all around and plow your field ready, then thereafter you may set up a home.

Do not be a needless complainant against your friend, when instead you can smooth things over with your lips. Do not say: What he did to me I shall do to him, to give each person what he deserves.

I passed by the field of a sluggard, and by the vineyard of this lackadaisical man. They were full of weeds, covered with thorns, and the stone fence had toppled. I gazed and gazed and gained a heartfelt lesson: A little more sleep, a few more winks, some more lazyboning in bed, and you may end up as poor as when you were accosted by an armed robber.

Chapters 25 through 29 again feature the basic one-verse proverb.

Chapter Thirty

T HE WORDS OF Agur bin Yakeh (Solomon), the oracle of the God-is-with-me person, God is with me and I succeed.

I am dull and without edification. I did not study wisdom, thus I do not understand things sacred. But has anyone ever reached heaven and returned? Did anyone ever capture the winds with his sleeves, or contain the seas in his straitjacket, or construct corners about the globe? Do we know his name and his family? We know only God's pronouncements and His dedication to those who believe in Him. Do not dare go beyond his pronouncements lest He punish your misdemeanor.

O Lord, I ask merely Two things of You in life. Keep me from emptiness and falseness, from both Poverty and Wealth, just give my daily bread. Lest I turn self-satisfied and defy the Lord, and lest I become impoverished and take the name of the Lord in vain.

Do not tattle on a slave to his master, or he may curse you for your wickedness.

A generation which curses fathers and refuses to bless mothers, a generation which acts holy but is filthy dirty, a generation which considers itself high and mighty, is the generation which has sword-like teeth and knife-life molars for eating up the impoverished people of the earth.

The leech has Two daughters, named Gimme and Gimme.

There are Three things which never fill, even Four which never get enough: The grave, penetrations of the womb, the globe never fills with water, and fire never says enough.

The man who looks askance at his father's husbandry of his mother, should have blackbirds peck out his eyes and the vultures devour them.

Three things are too wondrous for me, even a Fourth which I cannot fathom: The flight of an eagle in the sky, the way of a snake over the rocks, the path of a ship across the sea, and the way a male gets to his maiden. Then too, the way a woman has an affair, wipes herself clean, and says she has done no evil.

Three things cause revulsion in the land, and a Fourth which is intolerable: When a slave becomes king, when a low-life eats his fill, when a willing wife is despised, and when a maidservant turns mistress.

There are Four small beings on earth which are very smart: Ants are not much but they organize a food supply in summer, badgers are not a mighty specie but they place their homes in stone, locusts have no king but they advance in perfect formation, the spider crawls on its hands so it is there in the halls of kings.

Three beings advance with grandeur, even a Fourth that moves with pomp: The lion is the mightiest animal and will retreat before none. Thus too, the bull and the stag. Finally, a monarch – do not approach! If you offended redeem yourself, and if you contemplate an outburst, put hand to mouth. Because when you stir milk you get cheese, and when you strike a nose you get blood, and when you stir tempers you get quarrels.

Chapter Thirty-One

THE WORDS OF King Lemuel (Solomon), the oracle in which his mother reprimands him: My son, whom I bore, for whom I prayed, do not expend your energy on womankind, in the pursuit of princesses. And Lemuel as king, kings should not be wine drinkers, as no ruler should be a drinker of liquor. Lest he become drunk, forget the constitution, and disregard the rights of the downtrodden. Give liquors to the desperate and the wines to embittered souls. Have them drink to forget the poverty and their malaise. As for you, speak out for the unrepresented and provide justice for those who are oppressed. Open your mouth for the just rights of the poor and impoverished.

Faith personified

Seek and you shall find the valiant woman who is more precious than diamonds. Her husband will have full faith in her, as he turns richer with her every move. She will treat him magnificently all her living days.

She purchases select wool and linen, and fashions her clothing handily. She shops the international shippers that import the choicest foods. She was up before daybreak to provide for her family and to instruct the maidservants. Then she negotiated the purchase of a farmland and had a vineyard planted there. Still energetic, she rolled up her sleeves to help cultivate. Upon realizing that each of these undertakings were succeeding, she kept the lights burning late. Staying with her sewing, she took the weaving and darning needles in hand. Yet, she would hand a coin to a beggar and contribute to a charity cause. Her own family is ready for winter's snows, with their red flannel woolens. Their bedding and outerwear both come in linen and royal blue. Her husband stands out handsomely as he sits down with the city elders. She arranges for a belted cloak to be fashioned by a master tailor. She is dressed beautifully aristocratic, with no concern about tomorrow's trends. When she speaks one hears both wisdom and teaching of kindliness, as she checks on her family's manners, saying that no lazybones get to eat. Her children are the first to praise her, while her husband glorifies her, saying:

"There are many leading ladies out there but you surpass them all."

Glamor and beauty are misleading, while it is the God-fearing woman who deserves the honor. Let her enjoy the rich fruits of her enterprise, as her own accomplishments lead the applause.

II.
PSALMS OF WAR

Psalm 108

A *song with lyrics by David:*

Lord, my heart is ready and eager,
I can perform the song that's right,
Playing the harp and lute at dawn,
To show my gratitude to You internationally,
Because Your kindness is broader than heaven.
Lord, place Your glory on heaven and earth,
Respond to me with mighty redemption,
For You voiced Your sacred promise,
That I shall take over Shechem and Succoth,
That I will control Gilead and Menashe,
That Ephraim and Judea be my headquarters,
That Moab shall be my water basin,
That I'll use Edom to store our boots,
That I'll shout out my victory over Palestine.
But how can I overrun the fortress cities,
Now that You've abandoned us, O Lord,
And refuse to join our military?

Come save us from our attackers,
For the support of mankind is worthless,
With the Lord alone can we be victorious,
When He is there to crush our adversaries.

Psalm 83

A lyric poem by Asaph:
Lord, be not silent, don't hold back,
Because Your enemies are conspiring,
They who hate You are raising their heads.
It's against Your nations that they scheme,
With a final solution for the chosen people.
Announcing: We shall destroy this blood
So the name of Israel will disappear.
They are all allied for such an action,
An axis of evil aimed at the Lord:
The Europeans, the Arabs, the Bedouin and Egypt,
The Jordanians, the Nazis, the Palestinians and Lebanese,
The Iranians with their arms of mass destruction.
Lord, treat them like Midian, old Sisra and Yavin
At Kishon wadi, reduced to fertilizer for En-dor,
Treat them like old Orev, Zeev, Zevah and Zalmuna,
Who had planned to annex the territories of God.

Now treat these too like straw in the wind,
Like mountain forests going up in flame,
Pursue and confound them with storms and tornados,
Stuff them with shame 'til they cry out Your name,
Terrorize them with disgrace to their dying days,
When they may learn that You run this world.

II Samuel 22

David recited this song for God,
When God saved him from his foes,
And from Saul:
God is my rock, my fortress, and my haven,
My stronghold, my power, my trust, my shield,
The trumpet for my victories, and my protector.
I address God with praises and He saves me
From attack. When choking from calamity,
Frightened by a rush of outlaws, surrounded
By the dread of Hell, confronted with entrapment,
I turn to God in my troubles and pray.
From His sanctuary He hears my voice,
He lets my pleadings reach Him.
The earth then starts to shake in fear,
The mountains trembling at His displeasure.
Breathing fire, His mouth emits flames,
He lowers the heaven and descends,
With darkness clothing His footsteps.
He mounts a Cherub and flies on wind,

Encased by night, with cloud as armor,
His splendor pierces the dark in flame.
God's voice thunders from the sky in hail,
His arrows, forked lightning, confound the foe –
O Lord, Your whispered roar stirs the oceans
And bares the world's foundations –
He rescues me from a dangerous foe,
An enemy who is more powerful than I,
He advances and leads me into battle,
Nudges me to safety, because He likes me.
God is rewarding me for righteousness,
And for having hands clean of sin.
Following God's ways, I eschew wrong,
I am mindful of His Laws always,
And am honestly aware of my temptations.
So God repays according to my innocence.
For the pious there is kindness,
For the good man there is goodness,
For the crude there is cruelty,
For the crook there is damnation.
Thus, God, You rescue the poor people,
But dash the haughty to the ground.
You light my lamp, dispel the darkness,
I sweep thru enemy lines, unharmed,
You help me get over the embankment.
God's paths are perfect, His word is sure,
He defends those who depend on Him.
Is there divinity except for God's?

Or a fortress outside our Lord's?
You prepare me for certain victory,
My feet run uphill swift as a deer,
You train my hands to wage war,
For my arms to bend the metal bow,
You lend me Your protective shield,
Humbly projecting me as a superpower,
My steps proceed assured, not tripping,
I pursue the enemy, search and destroy,
Crashing him down at my feet.
O Lord, it is You who made me mighty,
Who let me overpower my antagonists,
Who made them run from me in tatters,
They prayed to God but got no answer,
So I mashed them and threw them to the wind.
You sustained me in quarrels with my men,
Then foreign peoples had to serve me,
The nations obeyed, cringing and lying,
And I let them stew, restricted to their capitals.
God lives, my blessed defender on high,
The almighty God who grants me my revenge,
Who puts the multi-nationals at my disposal,
Who saves me from armies and from terrorists.
This is why I glorify You around the globe,
Singing this song to Your divine name,
For magnifying the successes of the monarchy,
For being munificent with the anointed king,
With David and with his children forever.

Psalm 52

A *choral response by David, after Doeg of Edom told on David, telling Saul, "David is at Achimelech's house."*

Don't rejoice yet over this evil, big man,
For there's God's goodness at the end of the day.
But you have sought out words that hurt,
Like a razor blade behind one's back.
Always you loved evil and slander
Instead of kindness and speaking justly.
So because you espouse destructive gossip,
The Lord will crush you and demolish your home,
Uproot you from the living earth forever,
And the onlookers will worship and laugh:
That's the man who put not his faith in God
But trusted the supposed power of his wealth.
As for me, I always trust in God's kind works
And am like an olive grove in God's temple –
In the presence of Your worshipers, I shall
Constantly give thanks to Your good name.

III.
TORAH AS SONG

Jacob Blesses His Sons

(*Genesis 49*)

J ACOB CALLED HIS sons and said: Gather around and I
shall declare for you what finally will happen with you all.
Come, O sons of Jacob, and listen to your father Israel.

Reuben, you are my firstborn son; you embody my early vigor
and are deserving of primogeniture's bounty and authority. But
you became as whimsical as floodwaters and thus you shall not
lead. For you did intrude onto your father's couch and sinned.
Yes, he intruded onto my couch.

Simeon and Levi are a brotherhood, an alliance based on violence. My soul is revolted by their schemes, I dare not dignify
their pow-wows. In their rage they murdered a man, and for
a whim they smashed a city. Cursed be their rage which is so
explosive, and their hate which is so insistent. I shall divide
them amidst Jacob and scatter them throughout Israel.

Judah, it is you whom your brothers will glorify, because you
can contain the enemies. Then let your father's children all

make obeisance to you. Judah my son stands like a young lion after a kill. When he stretches out to rest, lion-or-lioness-like, none dares disturb him. Never shall the royal scepter be wrested from Judah, nor the rule of law from his grasp, when ultimately he achieves tranquility, as the multinationals collect around him. He hitches his steed at the vineyard and his little donkey at the orchard, with his jacket awash in wine and his overalls in grape nectar, his eyes sparkling from vintage and his teeth white with milk.

Zebulun shall dwell at oceanside with ocean-going vessels, stretching until the port of Sidon.

Issachar is like a pack mule crouching near the borders. He discovers that tranquility is best and that his land is fertile. So he bends a shoulder to the task and earns the profits of labor.

Dan will demand justice for the people, on behalf of all the tribes of Israel. Compare Dan to a serpent – a rattlesnake along the path – that strikes at the horse's foot and throws the horseman over.

O Lord, I seek Your help!

Gad will mobilize battalions who will drive off any foe.

From Asher come rich provisions, providing delicacies fit for a king.

Naphtali is like a racing hind that excites rousing applause.

A prolific individual is Joseph, a virile youth at a spring-well with the girls strutting about the plaza. But dangerous men threatened him with attack in a war of hate. He responded with overwhelming archery, whirling his mighty hands, hands empowered by his father Jacob, the essence of Israel's security. It was your father's Divinity who saved you, the Almighty God who blesses you. Blessings from heaven above and blessings from deep in the ground below, blessings for blessed breasts and wombs. These blessings of your father's surpass my own parents' blessings, with a love mightier than the universal mountains, and which now descend upon the head of Joseph, a crown for the prince among brothers.

Benjamin is like a ravenous wolf, consuming game each morning and dividing up the spoils each evening.

These then are the Tribes of Israel, twelve in number, and this is what their father said to them, blessing them, and giving each the fitting blessing.

The Song of the Sea

(Exodus 15)

Moses and the Children of Israel sang these lyrics to the Lord:

I sing to The Lord on His great victory, flinging cavalry-man and horse into the sea. Yes, I may sing my adulation to God because He did save me. He is my God and I applaud Him, the God of my forefathers and I extol Him. God is the name, yet He is a man-of-war: He has cast Pharaoh's chariots and infantry into the sea, drowning their generals in this Red Sea. All of them disappeared under water, dropping to the bottom like rocks.

O Lord, Your might is beautiful in its power, might which crushes the enemy. It is Your magnificent glory which overwhelms opponents. When You release Your anger, they burn like straw.

With Your breath You instructed the waters and had them stand up like liquid walls, solidifying the ocean deep. So that our enemy thought: Let me give chase, catch them, and fill myself with their booty. I will unsheathe my sword and force them to strip.

O Lord, You blew at the attackers and had the sea swallow them up, making them sink like lead in the stormy water.

O Lord, which mighty hero can compare to You? You are incomparable, graced by holiness, and eliciting awesome praise for working wonders.

You pointed with Your hand and the earth swallowed them. Then You showered with kindness this nation which You have freed, to lead it in safety toward the sacred homeland.

Those populations heard and squirmed, fear filled the Philistine inhabitants, Edom's military turned confused, the strong men of Moab trembled, all the Canaanite settlers became afraid. Anguish and terror enveloped them in facing Your mighty force. They stood stone-still, so that Your nation could advance, so that Your chosen people could march on.

You lead it to settle it atop Your birthright mountain, the palace designated for Your residence, the Divine Sanctuary which You build. May the Lord reign forever and ever!

All this when Pharaoh's horses, chariots, and cavalry drove into the sea, where the Lord doused them with the sea's waters, and the Children of Israel walked on dry land in the midst of the sea.

T HEN THE PROPHETESS Miriam, the sister of Aaron, took her tambourine in hand, and all the women followed her with their drums to dance. Then Miriam led them in song: Sing to the Lord upon His mighty victory, dunking horse and horseman into the sea.

The Song of Moses

(Deuteronomy 32)
Heaven and earth, hear what I say,
Spread the word like your rain and dew,
Like storms over meadow and showers on lawns;
Because it is God's name I proclaim,
Let us show the reverence that's due:
The Lord's work is always perfect,
He is correct in His every way:
True, unfailing, righteous, and just.
The holocausts you ask? Not His fault
But the fault of His children,
In decadent and corrupt generations.
Would you blame God, you low fools,
When He is your father and founder
Who created and nurtured you?
Think back to the Beginning,
Then examine the course of history,
Ask parents and elders who will tell you:
When the Lord apportioned the nations,

When the Lord distinguished the races,
He did so for the few Israelites,
Because the Lord wanted His people,
The Jew was His chosen lot.

He discovered them in the wilderness,
In the wild howling abyss,
He befriended them and enlightened them,
Guarding them like the apple of an eye.
Like the eagle rousing its brood,
Hovering gently over its chicks,
Extending its wing to lift them,
Then carrying them on its back.
So God too placed His apart,
Beyond the reach of any foreign power,
Transporting them to the heights,
Feeding them the fruit of the land,
Providing honey and oils amid the rocks,
Milk and cream from cattle and sheep,
With choice cuts of lamb and rams of Bashan,
Golden grain and luscious wine grapes.

But the Israelites grew fat and insolent;
Became opulent, muscular, rebellious;
They abandoned the Lord, demeaned Him;
They pained Him with idols and abominations,
They sacrificed to ghastly divinities
That their patriarchs would not recognize,
And forgot the Lord who gave them life.

God, enraged by His children, groaned:
I will hide my presence from them,
Let's see if they can endure –
These rough youths without manners.
They intimidate Me with false gods,
I will intimidate them with barbarians.
My anger is a fire reaching hell,
Consuming the earth, with its greenery,
And engulfing the steepest mountains.
I shall mobilize terror against them,
Together with the rest of my weaponry:
Hunger, fury, goblins, mad dogs and rattlesnakes,
Death by the sword outside, fear inside,
For boy, girl, infant, and the aged.
I thought: Damn them, let's erase
Their names from the memory of men . . .

Were it not for the ready antisemites,
Lest they claim a victory, saying
"We win," whereas God lets them.
They plan evils but understand nothing,
For if they were wise they'd ask:
How could one man defeat a thousand,
Or two men trap a population,
Unless their Lord sold them out?
But they do not know our Lord,
Because our enemies are idolators,
Their roots are in Sodom, in the fields

Of Gomorrah growing poison grapes,
For wines like snake's venom.
The Lord has the evidence against them,
To exact a condemnation when the time comes,
And their downfall comes swiftly now,
On the day God seeks justice for His people,
When He sees it powerless and in despair,
Taunted: "Where is the God you trusted,
Who received your sacrifices and libations?
Let Him bestir Himself to save you!"

"Here I am, I myself alone,
Am come to slaughter and to heal,
And nothing will stand in my way.
I now raise My hand to Heaven
To swear by My own eternal being,
That I'll not drop the blade of my sword
Until I take revenge on the enemy;
My arrows will find blood, My sword flesh,
Of the leaders of the pogrom hordes."
The world will cheer God's people,
When He avenges the spilled blood of His servants,
Repaying their enemies with just deserts,
And cleansing His land and His nation.

Moses Blesses Israel

(Deuteronomy 33)

Moses, the man of God, blessed the Children of Israel before his death, as follows:

THE LORD HAS come by way of Sinai, Seir, and Paran, arriving with a million angels and bearing a flaming Faith in His right hand. Here too is the favored nation, with all its holy men in attendance, throwing themselves at the Lord's feet and accepting His authority, by stating, "Moses has taught us the Torah and the tradition of the house of Jacob." So here are the King Divine and the nation's leaders assembled, all the Tribes of Israel together.

Long live Reuben, never die, and may his population multiply.

And for Judah, he said: O Lord, listen to the cries of Judah and bring him home safely. His armies will be victorious when You help him vanquish his foe.

And for Levi, he said: O Lord, grant Your revelations to this devotee, whom You tested in the wilderness and admonished over stormy waters. He can brush aside a father and mother, be a stranger to his brothers, even disown his own children, in order to obey Your commandments and to keep Your covenant. He can teach righteousness to Jacob, teach Torah to Israel. He is the one to place frankincense before You and a burnt offering on Your altar. O Lord, bless his fighters, granting success to their every maneuver, smashing the underbelly of the enemy so he can never rise again.

For Benjamin he proclaimed: God loves him, God is with him always, hovering over him all day long and resting between his peaks.

As for Joseph, he declared: May the Lord bless his land with the riches of heaven's dew and the flow of underground rivers. With the riches of sun-ripe grain and the riches of succulent nightshades, from the tops of ancient mountains to the terraces of timeless hills, with the bounty of a fertile land. All this, because he finds favor with He Who Descended To The Thornbush. May all this crown the head of Joseph, a prince among his brothers. As handsome as a thoroughbred steer, like a stag with twin antlers with which he butts away to land's end – these antlers representing the armies of Ephraim and the divisions of Menashe.

To Zebulun he said: Enjoy the success of your ventures, Zebulun, while Issachar tends the home office. Now call your agents back to a mountain retreat to render the thanksgiving offering, for they amassed profits from overseas, gathering the treasures of distant shores.

For Gad he said: Blessed be He who gives Gad his space, where he lives lion-like, tearing at heads and shoulders. He took first choice in a land of fabled wealth, having won the approval of the nation's leaders, and doing what is right and just before God and Israel.

For Dan he said: Dan too is like a young lion, romping through the Bashan.

For Naphtali he said: A happy man is Naphtali, in the possession of the lakes down South.

And for Asher he said: Asher is like a lucky boy, the delight of his brothers wading in rich deposits of oil, and with iron and copper in the foothills. Asher never has a bad day.

O Righteous People, there is none like the Lord, your defender who comes a-whooping, riding the heavens like a bronco. He is the overlord of the forces of creation and the underpinning of the universe's base. He can repel the challengers who confront you, letting you merely give chase, in order to settle Israel securely – alone around Jacob's water source – in a land of wheat and wine, under a sky dripping with dew.

O Fortunate Israel, there is none like you, a nation protected by God's proud sword and shield, so that your foes shrink before you, while you trample their embankments.

IV.
LYRICS FROM SPAIN

Ode to Zion

by Judah HaLevi

Ah, Zion, do reach out to your missing people,
These patriots who are your surviving nationals,
Who offer greetings from East and West, North and South,
With the greetings of a prisoner of hope, myself
Who sheds wet tears like the dews of Hermon,
While wishing to be shedding them on your peaks.
I moan here like a jackal over your misfortunes,
Then turn into a singing harp on dreaming your restoration.

My heart is in Beth-El pulsing before God,
In Mahanaim, in each splendid neighborhood
Where the Divine dwells in you,
For your Architect set your gates facing heaven.
The glory of God alone is your light source,
Not sun not moon not stars.
I am ready to pour out my soul
Where the spirit of God lingers about you.

For you are a palace, a throne in honor of God –
But how came slaves to the seats of your masters?
Still, I long to wander where the Lord
Was revealed to your seers –
Who can make me wings? I fly off
To lash my heartstrings to your precincts.
I fall to my face on the ground,
Delight in your dirt and stones.
Even more when at the graves of my fathers,
In a daze at Hebron beside precious tombs;
At Har Avarim and at Hor HaHar,
The burial plots of Moses and Aaron.

Your atmosphere is food for souls,
Your dust is spice, your rivers flows of fragrance.
I would treasure hiking even barefoot and bare
Through your ruins, your former castles,
At the place of your hidden ark
With the Cherubs in your sanctuary.

I cast off the pride of my accomplishments
To curse the Babylonian epoch
Which first desecrated your citizens.
For how can I enjoy my eating and drinking
When I witness dogs chasing your lions?
How can I enjoy the sunlight
When it shows vultures pecking your flesh?
Oh, cup of sorrow, relent
Because my body and soul overflow with poison:

When I remember fallen Israel, I drink this bitterness,
And recalling Judea captured, I swallow the dregs.

Beautiful Zion, you excite love and joy;
Bound to you are the lives of your friends,
Those who glorify your successes,
Who hurt at your pain,
Who weep over your destruction.
From prison dungeons they reach out to you,
Bowing from their distances toward your gates:
Your multitudes, driven like sheep everywhere,
But who will not forget your territories,
Who cling to your boundaries,
And struggle to climb your date palms.

Could Babylon or Egypt compare to your majesty?
Or their rituals to your sacred rites?
What compares to your kings, prophets and Levites?
The appeal of pagan nations will fade,
But your Rock is eternal, sanctity unto generations.

God desired you for His residence;
So blessed is he who perseveres,
Who goes to live in your countryside.
Blessed the person who awaits your rising star,
Your sunrise glowing about him,
To see the cheer of your champions,
To join in your celebration
When you reclaim your former splendor.

Earthling

by Abraham ibn Ezra (born 1089)

Every person born on earth
Knows he will end up in dirt.

The five-year-old is told he's great,
Every day getting bigger and bolder,
But spends his time at mother's breast,
Or rides around on papa's shoulder.

Every person born on earth, knows he will end up in dirt.

What can you teach a ten-year-old?
He's too young for serious training.
You make nice so he will listen,
His ma and kin are but his plaything.

Every person born on earth, knows he will end up in dirt.

Life is wonderful for the twenty-year-old,
He bounds like a buck over a hill,
He has no use for strict instructors,
He seeks a girl with looks that kill.

Every person born on earth, knows he will end up in dirt.

By thirty he is a woman's man,
Realizing that he's been trapped,
Surrounded now by powerful forces,
His children's needs and his wife's love-tap.

Every person born on earth, knows he will end up in dirt.

Fully harnessed, he reaches forty,
Satisfied with his inevitable situation,
Set in his ways, needing no friends,
With his only devotion to the work station.

Every person born on earth, knows he will end up in dirt.

At fifty he thinks of life as futile,
The thought of death will leave him crying,
The whole world's gold is worth a zero,
When one looks toward the time for dying.

Every person born on earth, knows he will end up in dirt.

"What's happened?" asks the sixty-one-year-old,
Because his life's work has had no meaning,
His true good deeds were few and feeble,
He whispers his protest instead of screaming.

Every person born on earth, knows he will end up in dirt.

If he makes it to the seventies,
Nothing he can say is considered serious,
He is a humbug to the friends remaining,
And the state of his health leaves him delirious.

Every person born on earth, knows he will end up in dirt.

At eighty he is a burden to the children,
He cannot manage nor see his way,
Scorned by the family, a joke all around,
His gourmet meals taste like hay.

Every person born on earth, knows he will end up in dirt.

So he would just as soon be dead,
But a lucky man knows that life is fleeting,
He expels illusion from his heart and head,
To dwell on his soul and the merit it's getting.

Every person born on earth, knows he will end up in dirt.

In Memoriam

AHARON BEN YECHIEL LICHTENSTEIN

Paris 1933–2015 Jerusalem